MW01267941

REAL ESTATE

BEST PRACTICES AND GREAT IDEAS

*Best practices and great ideas
to implement immediately
into your business*

Fran Cashion

ISBN: 1-4783-7695-3
ISBN-13: 9781478376958

REAL ESTATE

REAL ESTATE BEST PRACTICES AND GREAT IDEAS:

*Best Practices and Great
Ideas to Implement Immediately
into your Business*

Fran Cashion

To Dan, John, Elizabeth and Katy

I love you and thank you for your constant love,
support and encouragement.

Bessie —

all good wishes &
best of luck for continued
success —

Fran

Contents

Foreword

Throughout my real estate career, I have had the good fortune of interacting with many wonderful, professional REALTORS®. No matter what the market was like at the time, whether it be 18 percent interest rates, a plethora of short sales, or a multiple-offer market, real estate professionals continued to do a good and steady business.

Teaching and speaking gave me more exposure to agents who had great ideas about every aspect of their business. I made note of their suggestions, and also picked up ideas through "agent interviews," which I conducted prior to writing a class.

The "piece de resistance" occurred when I attended a national convention and the president of the organization asked us to text or tweet our favorite "best practice." I asked for a copy of these ideas, and received twenty-eight pages, single-spaced!

I compiled all these amazing ideas so that a wide audience of REALTORS® would benefit from them, build on them, make them even better, and more importantly, their very own, all to the enhancement of a better consumer experience for buyers and sellers.

This is not a "how to" book, but rather a "jumping off" book. It's a book of ideas to stir your creative juices and inspire and motivate you to change the way you currently do business if you want to improve and increase your productivity.

Once you have read through this book, highlight or make notes of what you consider to be the best ideas for you, and come up with an action plan. That is the best move you can make to take your business forward.

I hope "Best Practices" propels you to even greater success in your career!

Growing Your Business

....

Networking is not about hunting. It is about farming. It's about cultivating relationships. Don't engage in 'premature solicitation'. You'll be a better networker if you remember that.

– DR. IVAN MISNER, NY BESTSELLING AUTHOR & FOUNDER OF BNI

....

- Show up! Get up, get dressed, get ready, and go to the office every day. Treat your career like a "real job" and it will produce great results! This includes your home office, too.

- Listen more, talk less.

- Create a business plan and hold yourself accountable.

- Stop making excuses and devote time each day to prospecting.

- You must have a contact management program so that you can stay in touch with your sphere of influence on a daily, weekly, and monthly basis.

- Make a clear work schedule each week and then follow it. You will be more professional and get more work done as a result.

- Categorize your database beginning with your "Raving Fans," those people who will always refer you no matter what, then work your way through "B" and "C" category prospects, clients, and customers. Eliminate the "D" category. Add to your database every week.

- Keep a client log and pertinent information in your contact management program. This "jogs your memory" when you are having a conversation with them.

- Have a meeting with yourself every day, week, month, and year. Ask yourself, "How could I have increased my productivity and efficiency today, this week, this month, this year?"

- Commit to a daily goal of a specific number of people you will contact in some way to ensure the success of your real estate business. Don't end your day until it's done.

- Every day that you don't prospect, ask yourself why and refuse to use that excuse again.

- Set a daily goal to talk to ten people. Record who you talk to and follow up with a note.

- Join a BNI Group (Business Network International).

- Use Realtor.org for great industry information and ideas. Get familiar with RPR and House Logic.

- Be the "expert."

- Wear your nametag.

- Talk to all the people you know, and let them know what you do.

- Do fewer things, do them well, and do them consistently.

- Get familiar with all the tools your company offers and use them on a regular basis.

- Pick one new tool or technology to learn each week and become an expert.

- Get e-Pro certified and lose your fear of technology.

- Always give a little "extra." Give them what they didn't ask for. Surprise them!

- You are as successful as the people with whom you surround yourself.

- Get an assistant sooner rather than later.

- Set aside a separate account for taxes. After taxes are paid, save ten percent from every check.

- When in line at a drive-through restaurant, pay for the person behind you. It will make their day, and maybe they will pay your kindness forward. Ask the cashier to give them your card with a little note to "have a great day."

- Develop new homebuyer seminars via webinars or hold them in your office.

- Toward the end of every year, take a day, or a weekend, to plan your next year.

- Follow up with past customers/clients every month. Don't forget about them, no matter how small or large.

- At the beginning of the New Year, send a newsletter telling everyone in your sphere of influence that you will be calling them. This gives you a reason to call and is great motivation to pick up the phone and get through your entire list.

- You don't always have to speak directly to the person you are calling. Leave a message on the answering machine telling them you were just thinking about them. Do not mention real estate.

- Work toward a designation, or at least get more education than your state requires. Minimum requirements are never enough to excel in our business. Remember, most states require the person who cuts your hair to get 1200–1800 hours of education before they are licensed!

- Sponsor a baseball team. Provide magnets with the team name, your logo, and contact information.

- Follow up on every lead as if it were your only one.

- Volunteer at schools in your market area and get to know the teachers. They always know when someone is moving.

- Differentiate yourself from your competition by doing things your competition isn't willing to do.

- Listen to your clients and provide solutions to meet their needs.

- Talk to your local school and ask if you can supply water for the parents at some of the games. On game day/night, talk to people about anything other than real estate and really get to know them.

- When your buyer has completely moved into their new home, offer to have their first house warming party. Let them invite twenty of their friends. You provide food and wine/soft drinks. A great way to prospect for new clients while doing something nice at a small price.

- Go to garage sales to pick up listings.

- Join subdivision groups in your market area and go to the meetings and get to know the homeowners.

- Create video blogs with testimonials from past clients.

- Sponsor a garden club home tour in your market area.

- Hold a sellers seminar in your neighborhood. Send personal invitations and post a notice in a subdivision newsletter. Three months later, hold another seminar for buyers.

- Hire a Cub Scout/Boy Scout/Girl Scout Troop to decorate your neighborhood with flags on Memorial Day, Flag Day, and July Fourth. Put one in each yard, with your business card attached to the flagstick.

- Go walking in your farm area wearing your company logo shirts and always leave something of value (spring cleaning tips, information about an upcoming neighborhood event, etc.)

- Become a block captain on your street so that you are the "go-to" person for information.

- Include charity initiatives in your marketing and local presence.

- Use e-cards to make soft touches and stay in the mind of your customers.

- Keep up with past clients through postcards, e-newsletters, and phone calls.

- Print is not dead!

- After a sale, hold a house-warming party for your clients and invite all their friends and neighbors. Throw in some tickets to a local event for a drawing.

- Ask the neighbors if they know of anyone who would be interested in moving to the neighborhood. This really works.

- Become your neighborhood market expert.

- Mail "Just Listed" and "Just Sold" postcards to your entire sphere of influence, not just the neighborhood.

- See every person as a potential client.

- Send a competitive market analysis to past clients. It might take some time, but you will get referrals.

- Drive around once a week in your market area and jot down For Sale by Owner properties. Call them immediately, or better yet, visit them at their open house.

- Reach out and talk to people. Listen and follow up.

- Cultivate interests in areas other than real estate.

- You never have to bring up the subject of real estate, someone else will if they know you are in the business.

- Eat your "frog" first. In other words, do the tough stuff first and the rest of the day won't be as difficult.

- Be a professional, especially with your friends.

- Remember we are in a people business. Prospecting is a social event. It takes interaction. Be proactive. Make your contacts today. Don't wait.

- Get to know your neighbors. Walk the neighborhood. Talk about their interests.

- Get to know your children's friends' parents.

- Ask your clients while you are working a transaction with them, if they know anyone who wants to buy or sell.

- Host a cocktail party with a local lender for past and present customers/clients.

- Host a Super Bowl or other "theme" party for past and present clients, and ask them to bring their friends.

- Create an email signature.

- Establish a mastermind group of agents in your area to exchange information and ideas.

- If you haven't already, get familiar with Dropbox and Evernote to encourage a more paperless transaction.

- Host the big game! Is there a traditional rivalry in your area? Invite your clients/potential customers to watch the game and bring their friends. Give out pom-poms and make it a party!

- Offer to sponsor a local high school play. Print their programs in exchange for a back cover ad.

- Keep in touch with your rental customers.

- Wear company logo T-shirts while working out. Let everyone know what you do and why they need you.

- Work expired listings. You already know the owners want/need to sell.

- Make sure your hair stylist has your cards. They know all about their own clients and customers and they can pass along your information to potential buyers or sellers.

- Keep a stash of calendar magnets with your information and leave with your tip when eating out.

- Measure everything. Know what things cost and what business you get from each source. Remember you are running your own small company.

- Become a GREAT negotiator! It is a dominant facet of a successful real estate business and an attribute you should acquire if you have not already done so.

Open Houses

To be successful in real estate, you must always and consistently put your clients best interests first. When you do, your personal needs will be realized beyond your greatest expectations.

– ANTHONY HITT

■ For every Realtor out there, there are probably that many opinions about the value of open houses. Every locale is different. The key is to do what works and what your sellers ask you to do. If you hold open houses and you get business, keep doing it.

- Be pro-active with open houses. Invite a local author or artist and advertise as such, either a book signing or art show.

- Knock on doors or send flyers to invite a move-up neighborhood to an open house .

- When having an open house, be sure to have a competitive market analysis on hand for the subject property. Know the sold properties in case a neighbor asks questions or wants to list their property, too.

- At open houses, fresh flowers are a plus, but always make sure the lights are on and the toilet lids are down!

- When hosting an open house, have a gift basket with tickets to a sports function or some other activity, so that everyone who gives their contact information has an opportunity to win. This is a great way to have prospects give you accurate information.

- Have a twilight open house from 5-7 p.m.

- Adhere to local ordinances and Home Owners Associations rules as they apply to signage.

- Ask permission to place a pointer sign on someone's property and send a thank you note afterwards, including your card.

- Leave a note for the seller thanking them for the opportunity to hold their open house and inform them of the activity of the day.

Sellers

··

In a real estate man's eye, the most expensive part of the city is where he has a house to sell.

– WILL ROGERS

··

- Update your listing presentation and seller "interview." Know what your "conversion" rate is, and if it falls below 60%, review what you are doing with a peer or your broker. *See sample Seller Interview in the back of the book.*

- Never list with an unmotivated seller! "Why are you moving" is the most important question to ask on your listing appointment.

- Prepare pre-listing packets and deliver a day or two before your appointment, if possible.

- Call the day after closing, one week after closing, one month after closing, six months, and then yearly after closing.

- Listen to your clients and provide solutions to meet their needs. Buyers and sellers are asking us to be advisors, counselors and consultants.

- Learn how to differentiate yourself from your competitors. (What will you do that your competitors are unwilling to do?) Remember, it's not always the "big" things, but rather the "little" things that could make all the difference.

- The buyers who purchased your listing, may be potential customers, because most agents do not stay in touch with them after the sale. Make sure you do.

- Persuade tough sellers to use a stager. Offer to split the cost. Make a deal with the seller that if they listen to the stager and do what the stager says, and the house doesn't get a contract in 90 days, pay the other half of the stager fee.

- Send out custom e-cards with beautiful photos of your new listings.

- Put all listings in a subdivision newsletter with photos and highlights.

- Put your marketing plan online, so you can send to clients in advance as a link.

- Put your listing presentation on line with a secure password.

- Use solar lights on all your listing signs so buyers can see them at night. Your sellers will love it, also.

- When a seller asks about print advertising, ask them why it is important to them. You must understand the mindset of the client. Show them the advantages of social and business media marketing, such as YouTube, Facebook, and Linked In.

- Create a virtual tour of your client's home and put it on a DVD they can look at once they have moved. Create another virtual tour for your new buyer after they have moved in, and put on a DVD so they can use for insurance claims as proof of assets.

- Prepare a "Kids Listing Agreement" to engage the younger members of the family. Promotes keeping their rooms cleaned, toys picked up. *Sample agreement in back of book.*

- If the homeowner states what they owe, what they think their property is worth and how long they would prefer to list, they are a strong potential client.

- Do a thorough competitive market analysis for all listing appointments and present a phenomenal marketing presentation and package. Use resources like Focus 1st or Trendgraphix to create charts and graphs from information you download from your MLS. This helps sellers reach a pricing decision that will sell their house.

- Hire a professional photographer and a stager.

- Once the MLS information is published, review it and send it to your seller. This is the time to catch any mistakes or to enhance it with seller feedback.

- Include a generous number of pictures for each listing.

- Identify the rooms on your MLS pictures.

- For your new listings, host a weekday open house party for 10 or 15 neighbors to come at a specific time (4:00–5:30) to catch those working and those folks who don't want to come on the weekend.

- Tape an "information only" flyer to the underside flap of your flyer boxes. Buyers will always have critical information, even if the flyer box is empty.

- Present your contracts in person, if your MLS rules allow, and the seller grants permission for you to do so.

- When asking sellers for a price reduction, be prepared with the most recent specific, factual information.

- If your seller tells you to "take it off the market" during the winter months, you might explain that the winter months are when the supply side is down and their house might be the better house in winter.

- Always check the MLS for any errors immediately after you have entered a new listing. Fix any errors immediately.

- Don't let e-mail and automatic feedback take the place of phone calls to your sellers.

- Pre-inspections help sell properties.

- Provide constructive feedback to your fellow Realtors®.

- If the doorknob on your seller's home is not functional, or if the key sticks in the lock, have them buy a new front door knob/lock set. These small things are big things to the potential buyer and are usually the crucial "first impression."

- Host a "neighbors only" coffee on a Saturday morning when your new listing comes on the market.

- Be careful with the use of air or carpet fresheners because some people are allergic to them. It's better to make sure the place is super clean.

- Do some work to prepare your listing for showing before you put it on the market. De-clutter, de-personalize, add lighting and accessorize. If necessary, hire a stager.

- Get statistics on how over pricing loses money and pricing right makes more money and include the data in your marketing presentation.

- If you are having appraisal challenges, meet the appraiser at your listing prepared with detailed information the appraiser may not have. Don't forget that they do not have the opportunity to see as many homes as you do.

- Have a "Top Ten Things We Love about the House" flyer from the seller and place with your house brochures. This gives the buyers a warm and personalized "feel" for the property.

- Be aware of personality styles and follow the lead of your buyers and sellers as to whether they may be an analytical, social, director, or amiable personality. You cannot present in the say way to all four models, but rather you must take into account how they prefer you to present to them.

- Target-market your sellers home to homeowners/agents whose properties are 25–30 percent below the value of your listing to market to the move-up buyer.

- Send information on your new listing to the sales associates that have recently sold in your area.

- If your sellers want you to put up a "Do not let the cat out" sign, make sure you take a picture of the cat and post with the sign. Yes, there is a story behind this suggestion!

- Use additional sign riders for an open house, price reductions or a specific amenity (swimming pool.)

- Provide information to your sellers about the importance of putting their house on the market in its best condition in order to realize the best possible price. Touring currently listed properties with the sellers gives new meaning to the expression "a picture is worth a thousand words."

- Prepare your sellers for low appraisals.

- On the listing interview, prepare your sellers for a quick contract so that they don't immediately jump to the conclusion that their list price was too low.

- Remind your sellers that the "first offer is usually the best offer" and be prepared to negotiate all offers.

- The very best marketing plan is a "right priced" property.

- Market value is not determined by what an owner has put in a property, but rather what a buyer will get out of the property.

- Buyers determine the value of a seller's property by similar properties that have sold in the most recent time period.

- NAR surveys indicate that sellers feel most abandoned between resolution of unacceptable conditions and closing. Stay in touch those last few days by asking if they need boxes, reminding them of the closing time and place, making sure utilities are turned

over properly and reviewing the HUD state-
ment with them.

- A successful tool for listings is an interactive
  floor plan. Prospects can click on a camera
  icon in each room of the floor plan and a picture of that room pops up.

- Send the seller links to your "on-line" advertising.

Buyers

....

Real estate cannot be lost or stolen, nor can it be carried away. Purchased with common sense, paid for in full, and managed with reasonable care, it is about the safest investment in the world.

— *FRANKLIN ROOSEVELT*

....

- Pre-qualify buyer prospects 100 percent of the time – *Sample Buyer Interview in back of book.*

- Find out who is the real decision maker and you are 90 percent home. It is not always as it appears.

- Ask buyer/clients to meet you at the office. This helps you qualify them as serious buyers. Those who "can't make it" may not be ready.

- Tell your buyers to "bring your checkbook." This indicates you take them seriously about purchasing and you are planting the seed and the expectation that you are going to be successful in finding the property they want to purchase.

- Touch base with your buyers almost immediately after they move in and one month after they purchase, to see if they have any questions or concerns.

- Pay attention to the little things your clients say. Remember their favorite snacks or candy, or favorite restaurant. Surprise them with these special treats when you are with them, and with a gift certificate to their favorite restaurant after they close.

- Send your buyers a note of congratulations when they receive loan approval.

- Eliminate properties as you work with your buyers, and literally throw away any MLS sheet or other paperwork on properties they have rejected.

- Show buyers updates of MLS statistics indicating expired listings, back-ups, pending listings, and properties sold, to show them that houses don't stay on the market forever. This creates a sense of urgency.

- Alert your buyers to be careful about what they say in front of sellers or the seller's agent. If your buyer likes a property and provides positive feedback during a showing, the sellers could use this information during negotiations and it could prove detrimental to your buyers.

- If clients want to do something you don't recommend, get them to sign that they have been informed and are moving forward freely.

- Instead of "call me," try "text me."

- Bring a cooler with water for your clients on moving day (in and out) along with some sandwiches and light treats.

- Say "invest" instead of "buy."

- Treat all clients the same whether they are buying a $60,000 or $600,000 property.

- Send a "House Anniversary" card to all clients.

- Caution your buyers and sellers to keep their negotiations confidential until the transaction is closed. This is especially true for social media. Remember six degrees of separation. They do not want to compromise their negotiating position on Facebook or any other social media venue.

- Buyers have fears. They fear losing the property they love. They fear missing the "perfect" property after they write a contract. They fear they may pay too much. They fear they may not be working with the right agent. It is your job to allay all these fears through education, expertise and professionalism.

- Respect what buyers can afford and do not escalate their price point without their consent.

- Remind buyers that every house (even a brand new one) is a compromise.

- Help buyers see the possibilities in less than perfect houses.

- During the buyer interview, always give each buyer a blank sheet of paper and ask them to write down their three to five non-negotiable items. Typically, they will never be the same and you will have a better understanding of what each buyer desires in a property.

- Negotiation skills are a necessity in today's market. You need good negotiating skills not only to write the purchase offer, but also to negotiate the resolution of unacceptable conditions.

- Go find the house your buyer wants. It may not be in the MLS. Call in to the specific neighborhoods, or to homes that have their specific parameters, and ask permission to show their property.

Relocation Buyer and Seller Tips

....

It's tangible, it's solid, and it's beautiful. It's artistic, from my standpoint, and I just love real estate.

– DONALD TRUMP

....

- If you are fortunate enough to receive refer-ral business from a relocation management company, or local corporation, remember the importance of the source of these referrals.

- Make yourself aware of all corporate guide-lines by reading the instructions you receive from your relocation department and adhere to them.

- When providing a Broker Market Analysis to a relocation management company, remember that this information is going to a counselor who likely does not live in, or is familiar with, your city. Be their "eyes" and be honest about the property condition and true market value.

- Remember to always do your best to make the relocation management company "look good" to their corporate/government client. This is what a true partnership is all about.

- A relocating buyer has more than home-finding needs. They may need an area tour, information about schools, community activities, etc. Make sure you are an ambassador for your city as well as a great Realtor.

- A relocating individual or family is not only being affected by a move to a new city, but also changes will occur in their lifestyle, children's education, care for older adults, etc. Be empathetic with their situation.

- Be aware of the time constraints of relocating buyers. Some only have a weekend to purchase a property. Previewing properties before they arrive, conversing with them about properties they see on line, adds up to saving them time during their home-finding trip.

- Be aware of the instructions regarding who the seller should be on the contract, as well as other information that should be conveyed to the relocation management company as you are working through the relocation process.

- Turn in all reports on time. Your relocation management company counselor has to review these reports with their client corporations. Never put them in a position to say "I can't tell you anything about the property because I do not have an update."

- There are a myriad of forms not typical to the average local real estate transaction. Be familiar with them so that you can explain them in detail whether you are representing the buyer or the seller.

■ Thank your referral sources with personal notes.

Camera Tips

· ·

There are no rules for good photographs, there are only good photographs.

– ANSEL ADAMS

· ·

- Buy a good camera with a wide-angle lens.

- When photographing the front of a home, always make sure the sun is behind you. Sun-up to sundown are "magic hours."

- When shooting photos of kitchens with gran-ite counters, always shoot the photo with the counters between you and the windows so you can catch a reflection of the light in the granite.

- Invest in a DSLR camera with a wide-angle lens. A wide-angle lens will let you stand closer to the subject and show more of a room than just the furniture.

- Make sure the camera has a "hot shoe" attachment for an external flash

- When shooting indoors and you are facing a window, use your external flash attachment to compensate for the light coming through the window so as to tone down the window light. Overcast days are the best.

- One piece of camera equipment that separates the pros from the amateurs is a tripod.

- Stay up with the latest in camera technology. A WiFi enabled camera/camcorder will allow you to send photos and videos instantly to your computer, blog/FB, or e-mail. What a great way to service your newest listing!

- If you are farming a particular neighborhood or subdivision, take photos of all the activities in the area. They come in handy for brochures, websites, etc.

- Take photos of a previous listing to a new listing presentation. Explain how you use photography to sell a home. Remember, NAR states that 83 percent of all homebuyers look at web photos before ever contacting a Realtor.

- An elevated photo of the front of the home shows off the house at its best. Stand on a ladder, if possible, and if there is a tree close by, try to frame that in your shot.

- When shooting kitchens, set your tripod to the height of the countertop for a better effect and remove all items from counters.

- Remove all photos and magnets off the refrigerator door before photographing the kitchen.

- Remember the first photos a prospective buyer sees of your listing is your property's "handshake."

Closing Gifts

- Build attractive gift baskets, or use old-fashioned hatboxes. Among the items to include are bread, salt, and wine. The story behind those items is included in a letter to be placed in the box. It tells the story of something that takes place in a small town, in the 1946 movie, *It's a Wonderful Life*. In the movie, George Bailey, played by Jimmy Stewart, and his wife, Mary, played by Donna Reed, give a gift to an immigrant couple, the Martinis, who move into a new home in "Bailey Park." As they are standing on the doorstep during a housewarming party, they say these words as the Bailey's give the new homebuyers their gift. *"Bread – that this house may never know hunger. Salt – that life may always have flavor. Wine – that joy and prosperity may reign forever."*

- Have a wine bottler in your area? Create labels with one of your photos taken in front of the buyer's new home along with your contact information.

- Create a virtual tour of your client's new home and put it on a DVD and place it in a gift box.

- Purchase a subscription to a magazine that your buyer's will enjoy. They will think of you every month when they receive it.

- After closing, enroll your clients in a wine of the month club. It keeps your name constantly in front of them.

- While showing properties to your prospective buyers, or visiting with sellers during the course of their listing, listen for what type of gift might be most appropriate and something they will appreciate and remember you by after closing.

Personal Growth

· ·

Recognizing that you are not where you want to be is a starting point to begin changing your life

- DEBORAH DAY

· ·

- Visualize—see results in your mind before they happen.

- Make goals. Write them down. Reach for them every day. Reward yourself for achieving them.

- Write affirmations and read them every day. You are what you believe.

- Change your words and actions to reflect today's market.

- Plan your personal time off. This allows you to anticipate, recharge, and reinvigorate your business.

- Start each day with a clear and measurable goal. Know what a successful day looks like before your feet hit the ground.

- Give back to the community through projects like Habitat for Humanity.

- Luck is predictable. If you want more luck, take more chances, show up more often, and try more things.

- Understand what you do well and delegate or hire out the rest.

- Focus on your activities, not the results; the results will come.

- Volunteer, donate, assist those in need—it will always come back.

- Plan your time. Plan your learning. Plan your success.

- Count your blessings and keep a positive attitude.

- Schedule time off, take a vacation, and leave your business to a trusted sales professional.

- Read a business book a month and use one idea to apply to your business.

- At the end of every day, right before you go to bed, think of the three things for which you are most grateful from that day.

- Stretch yourself! Don't stay in your comfort zone.

- Everything we do is our responsibility.

- Your attitude affects how sellers and buyers feel. Don't forget, this is "show biz" and you are always "on."

- Outside influences should not affect your attitude!

- Don't let the business consume you. Have a life outside of real estate. It will provide real estate results.

- Treat everyone you come in contact with, the way they would like to be treated.

- At the beginning of each day, decide what you want to accomplish.

- Develop an amicable relationship, not an adversarial relationship, when working with a cooperating agent on transactions.

More Great Ideas

- Give back generously

- Decide what you want, write it down, and go after it.

- Own a smartphone.

- Find an "accountability partner" that you respect and hold one another accountable on a weekly or monthly basis.

- Once in the office, don't check your e-mail first thing. Make your prospecting calls and write your notes.

- Use apps that will support your business.

- Communicate with your clients based on how they communicate with you.

- Understand the decision-making process for each client and use it.

- Get proficient in expense management and tracking.

- Handwritten notes are not out of style—they produce calls back to say "thanks for the note."

- When sending Christmas cards, hand sign them and write a little note.

- You are in charge of your appointment schedule.

- Follow your instincts and drop clients that are wasting your time. If you don't like working with them in the beginning, it will only get worse.

- With the younger generations, texting and e-mail work best.

- Build a strong network of qualified professionals to provide advice and assistance to your clients and customers. Accountants, lawyers, credit counselors, and licensed contractors are just a few of the people you should know and be able to call on to get a client from contract to close.

- Use the word "you" instead of "I." Be the trusted guide, not the "know-it-all."

- If you don't have one already, create a website. If you don't know what a good one looks like, start researching your peers.

- Send birthday cards to your clients' kids.

- Video tape testimonials and include them on your website.

- Personal notes, followed up by a phone call, are an effective way to maintain a connection with customers/clients.

- Work hard to understand your customers/clients. What motivates them and de-motivates them?

- Limit your use of technology to things you can use properly and effectively.

- Never forget to thank people right away for sending you business.

- Invest in your business. Spend money to make money, but measure what you spend.

- Be proactive, not reactive. Surround yourself with positive and successful people. Maximize all of your potential and never give up.

- Develop a confident, positive attitude. People are buying and selling houses. It might as well be with you.

- Be an expert in your field.

- Have a good vacation agreement with another agent to allow you time to take off.

- Always have crayons and coloring books for small children.

- Carry a small drink cooler in your vehicle for water.

- Manage or own rental properties.

- Take classes, even if you think you know it all.

- Become knowledgeable about short sales and foreclosures. They will be part of your business for years to come.

- Host a client appreciation event.

- Prioritize when trying new things. Only start one new thing at a time. Once started, stick with it, either until it is an established habit or until you decide it is not worth doing. Then start something new.

- Always carry a flashlight and paper towels in your car.

- Don't forget thank you notes for lenders, coop agents, and closing officers.

- Take any and every opportunity to speak on an agent panel to share knowledge and expertise.

- Take opportunities to speak to civic organizations about your real estate market.

- Create a "How did we do" survey and send to all your clients. It will help you get better and it's another opportunity to touch your clients/customers and collect testimonials.

- Create a "blog" and make time to "blog"—your sellers and buyers will love it, as they see it as one more venue for you to promote their properties or find your buyers just the right home. After the sale, it allows you another way to touch them and provide good information about your current market, along with home "tips."

- With parents' permission, send a letter to the small children of your clients who have recently moved, telling them you have contacted Santa and given him their new address.

- Always, always, always, ask your buyers and sellers what is most important to them.

- Our customers/clients don't care how busy we are, they want us to take care of them.

- Be proactive in your communication. Don't make your buyers or sellers call you for an update. Ask your clients in what manner and how often they want to hear from you. Do they prefer text, e-mail, or phone calls? How frequently do they want to speak with you?

- Communication is critical. Knowing your clients' expectations is the only way you can meet them. Everyone is different, and they don't all require the same thing.

Reasons to Sell before You Buy

1.

Get your money
from sale of house in hand

2.

Increase your buying power
with no contingencies

3.

Reduce your fear of double house payments

4.

Secure the home of your choice
with no contingencies

5.

Rest assured your buyer's agent
will coordinate all the details

Advice to a Buyer
with a Home to Sell

Establish a realistic time frame

Consider monetary advantage
of selling prior to purchase

Look at your home
through a buyer's eyes

Remove clutter

Paint
(biggest bang for your buck)

Trim bushes

Remember,
you are not required to sell
until you are ready

Kid's Listing Agreement

Name:_____

Address:_____

I understand that my parents are trying to sell our house. (Your name) from (Your Company) is working with my parents as their Realtor. _____says that our house needs to stay as clean as possible so that a buyer will like our home.

In order to keep our house clean, I agree to:

⊗ Keep my room neat at all times.

⊗ Make my bed every day while our house is "For Sale."

⊗ Wipe my feet before coming in to the house so I don't track mud or dirt on the carpets.

⊗ Pick up all my toys, books, and games that I may use in the family room or basement or anywhere else in our house.

⊗ Put away my bikes, skateboards, and any other items I may use outside. I will not leave things in the yard or driveway after I am done with them.

If I do the things on this list, once our house has sold, I understand that I will get to choose something from the list below.

$20 Gift Card from (you choose the most popular "kids" places in your area....

Kid's Signature_____

Parent's Signature_____

Your Signature_____

The Buyer Interview

When the buyer is relocating:

1. Do you have some time to talk?
2. When do you plan on coming for your home-finding trip?
3. Are you familiar with our area?
4. Will you be moving with a family?
5. I will send you a relocation package. Is there anything in particular you would like to know about our area?

Buyer Questions – Personalize to the buyer's circumstances:

My goal is to help you buy a home that is right for you.

1. Tell me a little about yourselves?

2. What do you do in your time off? What do you do for fun?

3. Do you currently own a home or are you renting?

4. How long have you lived there?

5. How many homes have you owned?

6. How long have you been looking?

7. Have you seen any homes that you liked? (If yes, why didn't you buy?)

   If no, what are you looking for that you have not found?

   ° I've prepared a packet of information for you to take with you. It will help you understand the buying process.

   Have you been pre-approved for a loan? (If not, "we need to get started on that right away.)

   Will anyone be offering financial assistance?

8. What price range did you have in mind? How did you decide on that amount?

9. How soon would you like to be moved?

10. Why is that an important time frame?

11. How would your plans be affected if you moved (earlier or later)?

12. If we found the right home today, are you prepared to make an offer?

13. Will anyone else be involved in the decision to purchase?

14. (If they already own a home) Are you able to buy another home without selling your present home?

15. What are some favorite parts of the home you currently live in?

16. What attracted you to your home?

17. How did you start looking?

18. From the time you started, how long did the whole process take until you found the house?

19. Is there anything you would do differently?

20. How large of a home did you have in mind? Tell me more about that.

21. What style of home did you have in mind?

22. Help me visualize how you would like your next home to look?

23. What are the most important features to you? (Give each person a "must have sheet" to complete, and then compare their answers)

24. What are three things you can't live without?

25. What is the one thing you absolutely would not give up?

26. What requirements do your family members have? (Schools, etc.)

27. What hobbies and leisure activities should we consider?

28. Do you have any pets?

29. Do you have any special furniture you would like to accommodate?

30. How do you feel about cosmetic changes or repairs on a home?

31. How do you feel about buying brand new?

32. The last time (if there was a last time) you purchased a home, could you tell me about the process you went through to find that house?

33. How long do you plan on owning the property?

34. If the first home we look at turns out to be "your" house, how will you feel about that?

One of the ways I can tell if you like the home is to ask you if you would like to buy it. Is that okay with you?

Explain how you are going to select and show them homes. Explain For Sale by Owners and New Home Subdivisions

Stellar Seller Performance

1. Punctuality – Show up on time for all appointments. It implies courtesy and thoughtfulness.
2. Prepare a competitive market analysis which includes active sales, pending sales and expired sales. Come prepared with "sample histories" of properties that were over-priced in the beginning and have dropped their price dramatically or did not sell. Use absorption rate, charts and/or graphs compiled from MLS information.
3. Be the counselor/consultant and be prepared to coach and guide sellers in what they need to do to create a "marketable" product, including staging advice.
4. Demonstrate your commitment to pricing their property properly and, as indicated earlier, bring enough data to help them make an educated and informed decision. Be knowledgeable about Absorption Rates and the number of listings buyers would see in their price range.

5. Determine the seller's preference for communication and frequency of that communication and make sure you always communicate with ALL sellers in the transaction.

6. Be prepared to show your sellers how you connect with other Realtors in the marketplace because they control the "buyer pool."

7. Effectively market their property by using the latest in digital, high quality photos of their home for the MLS and brochures, as well utilizing internet marketing.

8. Tell your sellers that strong negotiation skills, especially in this market, are extremely important to bring the sellers the best possible price for their home.

9. Give your sellers an opportunity to accompany you to their competition to instill in them the importance of price and condition.

10. Inform and educate sellers about offers that come early, low-ball offers, and the importance of the "first offer."

The Seller Interview

(Sample questions)

1. Why are you selling your home?
2. Where are you moving?
3. When do you need to be there?
4. Do you need any assistance with that move? (if they need a referral to their destination city)
5. Tell me about any updates and improvements you have made to your property or describe your home for me.
6. How long have you lived in the home?
7. When you purchased this property, what attracted you to the home?
8. Have you worked with a Realtor before?
9. Tell me about that experience?
10. Are you willing to list your property at market value?
11. Do you have a price in mind?

Made in the USA
San Bernardino, CA
10 October 2013